T0285989

Also by Adam Zagajewski

True Life

Adam Zagajewski, *True Life*.
Translated from the Polish by
Clare Cavanagh. Farrar Straus
Giroux, New York.

Farrar, Straus and Giroux
120 Broadway, New York 10271

Copyright © 2019 by Adam Zagajewski
Translation copyright © 2023 by Clare Cavanagh
All rights reserved
Printed in the United States of America
Originally published in Polish in 2019 by A5, Poland, as *Prawdziwe życie*
English translation published in the United States by Farrar, Straus and Giroux
First American edition, 2023

Poems from this volume originally appeared, in slightly different form, in the
following publications: *The Threepenny Review*, *The Times Literary Supplement*,
Liberties, *The New York Review of Books*, and *The New Yorker*.

Library of Congress Cataloging-in-Publication Data
Names: Zagajewski, Adam, 1945–2021, author. | Cavanagh, Clare, translator.
Title: True life / Adam Zagajewski ; translated from the Polish by Clare Cavanagh.
Other titles: Prawdziwe życie. English
Description: First American edition. | New York : Farrar, Straus and Giroux, 2023. |
Identifiers: LCCN 2022044448 | ISBN 9780374601560 (hardcover)
Subjects: LCGFT: Poetry.
Classification: LCC PG7185.A32 P7313 2023 | DDC 891.8/5173—dc23/eng/20220919
LC record available at https://lccn.loc.gov/2022044448

Designed by Crisis

Our books may be purchased in bulk for promotional, educational, or
business use. Please contact your local bookseller or the Macmillan
Corporate and Premium Sales Department at 1-800-221-7945, extension
5442, or by email at MacmillanSpecialMarkets@macmillan.com.

www.fsgbooks.com
www.twitter.com/fsgbooks
www.facebook.com/fsgbooks

10 9 8 7 6 5 4 3 2 1

The true life is absent. But we are in the world.

EMMANUEL LÉVINAS

Contents

True Life

The Twentieth Century in Retirement

Let's try to imagine it:
a little like old Tolstoy
he strolls the fields of Picardy,

where funny tanks once
clumsily defeated
the terrain's slight elevation.

He visits the town
where Bruno Schulz died
or sits on a riverbank

above the Vistula's dim water,
a meadow scented with warm
dandelions, burdocks, and memory.

He doesn't speak, rarely smiles.
Doctors warn him
to avoid emotion.

He says: I've learned one thing
There is only mercy—
for people, animals, trees, and paintings.

Only mercy—
always too late.

Drottningholm

A photograph from years ago—my parents
outside Drottningholm Palace
near Stockholm.
It's probably September,
month of partings and rapture.

My father in his tie,
my mother's scarf
(elegance pre-1968).
They watch me closely,
fondly, with concern.

And higher, over them,
clouds, indifferent, deep blue,
and a little sun that illuminates
the tourists' silhouettes. Perhaps
it wants to enter their hearts.

The Great Poet Basho Begins His Journey

After lengthy preparations
the great poet Basho begins his journey.
The very first day he happens
to walk past a sobbing child
abandoned by his parents.
He leaves him by the roadside,
because, he says, such is Heaven's Will.

He walks on, northward, toward the snow
and things unseen, unknown.
Slowly the imperfect cities' sounds grow still,
only streams hold forth chaotically
while white clouds play at nothingness.
He hears an oriole's song, delicate,
uncertain, like a prayer, like weeping.

Santiago de Compostela

Light drizzle as if the Atlantic
were examining its conscience

November no longer pretends
Rain dowsed its bonfires and sparks

Santiago is Spain's secret capital
Patrols arrive day and night

Pilgrims wander its streets, exhausted
or eager, like ordinary tourists

A woman sat by the cathedral
she leaned on her backpack and sobbed

The pilgrimage is over
Where will she go now

Cathedrals are only stones
Stones don't know motion

Evening approaches
and winter

7 Arkońska Street

Mrs. Jodko, a beauty once, slowly
died of multiple sclerosis.
Mr. Zawadzki became an MP in the new regime
but we didn't hold it against him.
Wojtek Pszoniak lived on the second floor,
I lived on the third, I listened to the radio

and read *Captain Grant's Children*.
I loved Professor Paganel.
Mr. Jodko had a jeep from army surplus
(Wehrmacht): the scent
of gasoline enticed me.
Journeys smell like that, I thought.

The months came and left
discreetly, English-style.
But streets stood motionless
summer and winter, like statues
on Easter Island,
gazing in one direction only.

Boogie-Woogie

You shout from the other room
You ask me how to spell boogie-woogie
And instantly I think what luck
no war has been declared
no fire has consumed
our city's monuments
our bodies our dwellings

The river didn't flood
no friends
have been arrested
It's only boogie-woogie
I sigh relieved
and say it's spelled just like it sounds
boogie-woogie

Wicek Faber

Wicek Faber died young and left behind
a poem: *You're so funny underneath the window*
and Ewa Demarczyk sings these words
on different records, which spin quickly
but Wicek Faber hears nothing
(*as the cool dusk descends*).
For such is immortality,
ladies and gentlemen, careless, indifferent
and nothing to be done, dear friends
(*dark clouds loom above the city*
soon the rain will surely fall).

Stop

For example a quick stop
at a small beekeeping museum
midway between Belgrade
and Novy Sad; an August day,
—carefree, almost happy.

A beekeeping museum—what could be
more blameless?
There are no ministers
or rock stars here, in fact
even the bees have gone.

Or the moments following a reading,
when dailiness gradually resumes
and slowly, quietly you
become yourself again
—life may happen then too.

Miriam Chiaromonte

Miriam was like a small bird
who fears nothing.
Her memory was great
and she trained it systematically.
Each day she would learn a new poem,
for example, one of Shakespeare's sonnets.
She understood everything.
We thought she
might be immortal.
Alas we were wrong.

Mountains

When night draws near
the mountains are clear and pure
—like a philosophy student
before exams.

Clouds escort the dark sun
to the shaded avenue's end
and slowly take their leave,
but no one cries.

Look, look greedily,
when dusk approaches,
look insatiably,
look without fear.

Rain in Lvov

it falls on Wawel's dragon
it falls on giants' bones
TADEUSZ RÓŻEWICZ, "Rain in Kraków"

It falls on the Armenian cathedral
and on the Uniate Church of Saint George.
On the opera and on the black house.
Hills vanish in the mist.

And Ostap Ortwin, who
was a valiant man
(he defended Stanisław Brzozowski).
Shot on the street
by the gestapo.

Civilization has five syllables.
Pain—only one.
In London I saw van Eyck's self-portrait
inscribed "Als ich can"—that is,
"As best I can"—and it is not a selfie.

Rain falls on the Scottish Café
and on the High Castle
on the Kaiserwald
and on the synagogue.

And this city, which sat
on seven hills like Rome
with its scepter and orb
grew flat and small.

Tram wheels screeched
on their tight tracks.
And all of us wept
bypassers and guests
victors and vanquished.

Enlightenment

Poetry is civilization's childhood,
said the Enlightenment philosophers,
so did our Polish professor, tall, thin
as an exclamation point that has lost its faith.

I didn't know what to answer then,
I was still a bit childish myself,
but I think I sought wisdom

(without resignation) in poems
and also a certain calm madness.
I found, much later, a moment's joy
and melancholy's dark contentment.

Sambor

We drove through Sambor quickly,
almost instantly, it took five minutes.

But my mother, as I recall,
passed her exams here.

Dusk fell
without funeral marches.

A lone colt danced on the highway,
though it didn't stray far from the mare;

freedom is sweet,
so is a mother's nearness.

Over fields and forests
gray silence reigned.

And the little town of Sambor
sank into oblivion again.

The Allegory of Good and Bad Government

Good government, *Buon Governo,*
and the good judge—we see
how Siena thrives
under the just ruler.

Peace reigns over all, revealed.
The peasants work serenely,
grapes swell with pride,
a wedding party dances in the street.

But bad government sets out
to torment justice,
who bears the lovely name Iustitia,
it lies, it sows Discord,

it delights in Wickedness
and Deceit; it ends by hiring assassins.
The town empties, fields cease
to bear fruit, houses burn.

Still, after seven centuries, just look,
(compare the two frescoes)
evil is pale, barely legible
while Good compels our gaze
with its rich colors.

Only seven hundred years
of waiting.

Border

The scent of gasoline crickets
VLADIMIR HOLAN

Poor people wait by the border
and look hopefully at the other side
The scent of gasoline crickets
skylarks sing
the abridged version of a hymn

Both sides of the border face east
The north is east
And the south is east

One car holds a giant globe
showing only oceans

A little girl in an ancient Fiat 125
carefully does homework

in a green ruled notebook—
there are borders everywhere

Brief Moments

The brief moments
That happen so seldom—
Is this really life?

The rare days
When brightness returns—
Is this really life?

The instants when music
Retrieves its dignity—
Is this really life?

The few hours
When love prevails—
Is this really life?

Winter Dawn

It happens in winter, at dawn
that a taxi takes you to the airport
(another festival).
Half-awake, you recollect
that Andrzej Bursa used to live
right here, just outside,
he once wrote: *the poet suffers for millions.*
It's still dark, at the bus stop
a few people huddle in the cold,
seeing them you think, lucky souls,
you only suffer for yourselves.

In Drohobycz

But in some small towns
the shadows
are more real
than things

Evening also
arrives there
Old houses
calmly wait

Darkness comes next

See
how gently

Figs

Figs are sweet, but don't last long.
They spoil fast in transit,
says the shopkeeper.
Like kisses, adds his wife,
a hunched old woman with bright eyes.

And That Is Why

And that is why I paced the corridors
Of those great museums
Gazing at paintings of a world
In which David is blameless as a boy scout
Goliath earns his shameful death
While eternal twilight dims Rembrandt's canvases,
The twilight of anxiety and attention
And I passed from hall to hall
Admiring portraits of cynical cardinals
In Roman crimson
Ecstatic peasant weddings
Avid players at cards or dice
Observing ships of war and momentary truces
And that is why I paced the corridors
Of those renowned museums those celestial palaces
Trying to grasp Isaac's sacrifice
Mary's sorrow and bright skies above the Seine
And I always went back to a city street
Where madness pain and laughter persisted—
Still unpainted

Bolt

My grandfather taught the German course
at Lvov University—eight a.m.
Many students came late.
Grandfather Karol upheld discipline,
he screwed a dead bolt to the jamb
and at a few minutes past eight
the hall was hermetically shut.

But they slept on, long, happily,
and didn't know the town would vanish
along with the bolt, everything would cease,
then deportations, executions, grief,
and the bolt would become
a blissful memory,
a clasp from Herculaneum, a treasure.

Another Life

You like to read biographies of poets
You rummage through another life
That sudden shock
of entering another life's dark forest
But you may leave at any moment
for the street or the park
or from a balcony at night
you may gaze at stars
belonging to no one
stars that wound like knives
without a drop of blood
stars pure and shining
cruel

The Old Painter

The old painter stands by the studio window,
where his brushes
and colors lie.

Poets wait for inspiration, but objects
and faces assault the painter,
they arrive shrieking.

Their contours, though, have
blurred and faded.
Objects turn blind, mute.

The old painter feels only
a dim wave of light,
a longing for form.

And he knows even now
that he may see again
the bitter joy of indistinction.

We Wait

One afternoon
Alfred Cortot plays Chopin
but only on a record
So what
There is eternity
There is delicacy
and dark powers
that drowse
We all wait
what comes next
There is eternity
but it ends soon
Sounds are lightning strokes
they can't be stopped
We can be stopped
just like that
stop

Istanbul

I see those boys once more, in the afternoon
sun, how they pinch their noses
and jump into Istanbul's sea
from a low concrete embankment.
Then they came straight from the water,
shining like damp pebbles,
and jumped back in again—
as if there really could be *perpetuum mobile*.
I don't know if they were happy, but I
was, for a moment, in the blaze
of a May day, watching.

Self-Portrait Beneath a Drip

Mr. Zagajewski? the nurse checks.
Yes, I say, it's me.
The antibiotic is transparent
as spring water
and never hurries.
Outside the window I see an old ash tree,
it spreads young leaves
enjoys the air
and the May sun and the breeze.
Since the hospital on Sunday,
my friends, is not a hospital,
it is a promenade, a beach, an airport,
compote, cardiology, and sleep.
I also see the stadium, Clepardia sports club,
the blue team plays against the red,
and the red team plays against the blue.
But peace reigns here,
silence and transparency;
I keep out of the fight.

The East

Sunflowers with crumpled faces,
inquisitive beans ascend thin poles.
The idyll of deep gardens: roosters crow.
Suddenly there's Zamość, Leśmian's home,
then mallows bloom and you see Bełżec,
empty town inhabited
by half a million shadows, total silence of so many voices,
and no one cries now—just four
pretty Jewish girls from the Kolbuszowa ghetto
gazing for years at the camera as if it were salvation,
but there was and will be no salvation,
only the camera, there is and will be
the lens with its azure sheen
like alcohol set flaming in a glass,
and the little wooden churches wait for fire
quite calmly, without motion.
This is the east without sun, this is the sun
without summer, it's not far now
to final places, to origins, to the edge,
to black earth, to the aria with no end.

Kardamyli

Gałczyński in a prisoner-of-war camp:
never so devout before or after.

What can a person who is a poet do—
in the army, the hospital, or the world?

Refugees from Syria drown in the sea
or suffocate in refrigerated trucks.

In Kardamyli, a dead cat lay on the highway
(I just miss running over it)

—and why was I so grieved,
as if I'd lost somebody dear.

We're safe, hidden
in concrete boxes, in fear.

A north wind blows, the Meltemi,
figs drop on the earth's cracked mouth.

September 2015

Yoga of Voices in a Hospital Corridor

This is not Vivaldi or Stockhausen
These are untrained voices
This is not bel canto
You catch a whisper sometimes a curse
Or silence full of bitterness
Two old women
talk about the doctors
—The blond guy is politer
On a stretcher an old man with a white face
lies with eyes shut
There is no compassion here
compassion stepped out and won't be back anytime soon
it left no address

I'm Fifteen

I'm fifteen. I'm a boy scout,
I lost my knife and compass in the woods.
I walk along Dworcowa Street, high above me
Silesia's hazy sun and a hawk
who seeks a friend in vain.
I'm an altar boy in an ugly church,
I'm twelve, I know the sacristy's smell,
its blend of starch and sweat.
I listen to jazz, Charlie Parker is dead now.
I'm eighteen, I'm a high school graduate
in a white shirt and a navy tie.
I've started reading poetry, I sometimes
seem to understand everything.
I'm fifteen, I watch adults
indulgently. I'm certain I won't
make the same mistakes.

Wind

We always forget what poetry is
(or maybe it happens only to me).
Poetry is a wind blowing from the gods, says
Cioran, citing the Aztecs.

But there are so many quiet, windless days.
The gods are napping then
or they're preparing tax forms
for even loftier gods.

Oh may that wind return.
The wind blowing from the gods
let it come back, let that wind
awaken.

The Calling of Saint Matthew

that priest looks just like Belmondo
WISŁAWA SZYMBORSKA, *Funeral (II)*

—Look at his hand, his palm. Like a pianist's
—But that old guy can't see a thing
—What next, paying in a church
—Mom, my head aches
—Sharply individuated human figures
—Keep it down please, we can't focus
—The coins on the table, how much are they worth
—His operation's just three weeks away
—I'd say silver, definitely silver, but not pure
—Lord, how lovely
—To adorn the Contarelli Chapel
—Which one is Matthew, the young guy or the old?
—We almost got robbed on the subway today
—Two generations of European artists took it as their model
—Look, there's a cross in the window
—The light went out again
—The wall on the left is so black, like the world's end
—Have you got another euro or fifty cents?
—Can't be the young guy
—They're closing soon, hurry up
—He saw a man collecting taxes
—How much are these paintings insured for
—Jesus is in shadow but his face is light

—I'm leaving now, I'll wait outside
—Why don't they have a guard?
—They live in semidarkness and suddenly there's light
—It's going out

Three Caravaggio masterpieces hang in a side chapel of the Church of San Luigi dei Francesi in Rome; you put coins in a meter to turn on the lights.

Charlie

in memoriam C. K. Williams

Charlie announced once in New York:
we will be friends—and we were friends
for thirty years.

He was impatient, high-handed at times,
but he understood that only kindness binds.
Tall, with the face of a Spanish nobleman.

He headed for his study every morning
like a worker off to the vineyards
armed with great shears of imagination.

He wrote slowly, revised his poems time
after time—guiding a line of rapture
from thickets of dense prose.

He didn't seem poetic at first sight.
His father sold refrigerators and TVs
but a messenger approached him, spoke in whispers.

On summer vacations near Lucca he rose first,
and in the garden, in a white djellaba from Morocco,
he hunched over his black computer.

His grandmother told him she came from Austria,
but she was born in Lvov, before Ellis Island
her name was Grabowiecka.

Friendship is immortal and doesn't demand
many words. It is calm and patient.
Friendship is the prose of love.

Four days before he died he lay in bed, weak, wasted
like an Auschwitz prisoner with large dark eyes
awaiting liberation.

Where the Tamarisks Bloom

You didn't want to swim
where the tamarisks were blooming.
That beach is too *populo*, you said.
It's true, it was a bit *populo*.
Loud music blasted,
local pensioners played cards,
a provincial sun descended.
It should be noted though
that the tamarisks were blooming,
elegant, exceptionally fine,
and a green sea reigned,
endless, always promising more.
I swam for a while
and when I got out I saw
a turtledove sip water
from a puddle by the shower
and I thought that is
a sign of peace.

Córdoba, Sparrows

to Karol Tarnowski

All around the scent of orange blossoms
like a soft silk handkerchief;
here memory is stronger than time,
each day the cathedral must once more
seek refuge in the mosque.
Córdoba is this country's
black heart, the harsh judge
of invisible things, the judge of wrath
and joy, laughter and indignation.

Meanwhile tourists like divers
in wet suits stroll across the ocean's floor
seeking treasures, stirring unreal
clouds of dust beneath their feet.
And endless dusk lingers,
the endless May evening,
sparrows chatter loudly, shadows
return very slowly
to their dark apartments,
trees are seized by a light tremor,
even fear, as if they'd finally realized
that this is it, they have nowhere to go.
It might seem now

that a secret yearns to be revealed,
it shoots its hand up like the teacher's pet,
but we know this isn't possible.
Philosophers must choose their city,
only poets can live everywhere.

Journey to the Holy Land

An old bus took us eastward
in the afternoon

Kings in tattered cloaks
slept on narrow seats
like workers on suburban trains
heads drooping to their chests

The desert stretched

The season was uncertain

There were no prophets
They'd doubtless been arrested

We knew
it would be the same
as always

It would all go back to normal
Dirty police stations crumpled cash
Rage

But now
we were traveling to the Holy Land
Where there is joy

The sun rose
a pink scar
on the sky

André Frénaud

He spent a year teaching in Lvov.
Paris after the war, rue de Bourgogne,

a narrow street, quiet, perfect for poets
and contented bourgeois.

I liked his poem
"The Three Kings," and others too,

for instance, "House for Sale,"
which begins as follows

(as per Zbigniew Herbert's Polish version)
"Here lived many who loved" and it ends:

"Let's open the windows . . . Change the sign.
Someone enters, sniffs, starts over."

He lived in an old Parisian
stone building, where the parquet creaks,

and doors open with not handles but knobs
that gleam like mirrors, polished

by the fingers of those who "started over"
and those "who loved."

Carmen

Some girls even very young
dye their hair black
The results are not always becoming

This may conceal the call of Spain
the lure of tragic Carmen
a fury not available to all

I read poems by Adam Ważyk constructed
from cold indifferent images though beneath them
we sense a keen (and cautious) mind

It's a sunny day, images return
A cortege of Kraków residents
proceeds unhurriedly before me

Life files calmly through the Planty Gardens
quite pleased with itself all in all
Modest people walk leashed

miniature pinschers, mutts; small dogs prevail
Beside them thrushes like runway models
display their charms

At last it's May, famous May,
the month of promises
that nobody thinks to check later

A Provincial Roman Town

The town swept clean by archaeologists
no longer holds secrets.
Since they lived exactly like us.
They gazed at the sea each evening,
sipped sweet wine lazily,
and dreamed the same things we do.
They knew that dreams go unfulfilled.
They had their gods, quarrelsome, preoccupied,
neglectful. But there was also divinity,
hidden everywhere, invisible.
They tried to catch it in paintings,
in poems and melodies, without success.
The town plan was transparent as the dawn,
and the sun made its way without trouble,
summer and winter, always, daily.
They waited for barbarians, afraid,
raising ever higher walls and towers.
(But the barbarians never came.)
Time's light wagons crushed them,
the wheels ran swiftly, silently,
and still run.

CD

At Catherine's request I sent
a CD to Charles then.
It had Bach's Chaconne, Beethoven's
last piano sonata,
and Chopin's scherzos (nearly all the "music
you'd take to a desert island,"
assuming the island
came suitably equipped).
I know he listened to the disc
in his last days and maybe he thought
about leaving that wealth,
the happiness hidden
even in the saddest largo.

Sunday

Yes of course, go to church
on Sunday, at eleven
or twelve, in clean shirts,
carefully pressed dresses.
Go to church, you'll find

a priest with a fat chin.
He'll speak at length
in unimaginably lofty tones,
he'll tell you what to think and do.

God is elsewhere, elsewhere.
We know nothing. We live in darkness.
God is elsewhere, elsewhere.

In the Garage

And then when you entered
the empty garage
a trumpet called
as in the Fifth Symphony
And it suddenly grew clear
that there is joy and death
and mad flies
circling the table
where all of you sat
just moments ago
calmly chatting

Ezra Pound

A military plane
Transports him from one prison to the next

He is downcast apathetic

But when the great red ball
Of the setting sun appeared
Over the Atlantic
He danced ecstatically
To greet the light

We might think
His doctrine *make it new*
Was realized perfectly
This once

Homeless

My friends advise me
To stop grieving
You're not all that homeless
They say
         We know you lost
The other city but now after all
You live quite well
It could be worse

I agree with them how could
I say they're wrong

Then they leave happy
And I repeat:
You live quite well
You're not all that homeless

And I start believing
What my friends
Tell me

Instrument

Why do you write about music, what does
music mean to you, can you point to
the one instrument that most
inspires you, do you still listen to jazz,
why don't you play an instrument,
and what is music anyway, why can't you
say anything about it, do you think mysticism
still has a future ahead of it, and if so why,
and would you agree with the claim
for example that despair is beautiful?

Jean Améry

A person frail as any other

A frequenter of libraries erudite self-taught

He hated brute force

In each group portrait he is always
the slightest; as if he were slowly
exiting the photo

A hundred years hence he will be completely gone

In the Bayonne prison he tried
to understand quantum physics

He was tortured at Fort Breendonk

To his last day he tried to understand torture

He was self-taught in this field

We don't know how one can be a victim
Or an executioner

Everything else is easy
(or easier, let's say)

On an Island

The tracks on this island were torn up long ago
but their traces remain just the same

The little station still stands and two platforms which
have eyed each other for years—but never meet

A huge full moon rolls from under a cloud
and watches closely like one who comprehends

The tracks were torn up long ago but the road still exists
Roads cannot be destroyed

Even if peonies cover them
smelling like eternity

Bełżec

Summer ends, fall has not yet begun.
What a lovely day, the blackberries in the woods
must be dark as the lips of screen sirens in silent films.
And just then you see Bełżec.
Only cinders and grief remain, only quiet,
and sleepy occupants who
still wait for an answer.
The blackberries grow ever darker.
The shadows, hollowed, are black.
Burnt love is black.

Rembrandt, Self-Portrait 1629

Beneath a cloud of dark hair
a white lace collar
immersed in the coat's abysses
Lips parted
Everything is still possible
On the young face
fear of life
and certainty of triumph
(we know how misleading
these triumphs are)

Magnolia

And also that moment
when the black cat
sleeps on my knees
completely safe
and the magnolia blooms
on Kochanowski Street
and Franz Schubert hasn't died
and the Tartar arrow
misses Saint Mary's tower
(but then you wouldn't have
the trumpet call you like)

The Old Painter on a Walk

In his pockets treats for local dogs
He sees almost nothing now
He almost doesn't notice trees suburban villas
He knows every stone here
I painted it all tried to paint my thoughts
And caught so little
The world still grows it grows relentlessly
And yet there is always less of it

November

You stand by the music school
You hear a new generation practice
You hear chaos that grows
and makes promises
The city continues to deliberate
A flash of concentration and a sergeant's shriek
The botanic garden and the stock market's paper prices

You walk along a street that doesn't end
and on both sides
minor battles are waged
negotiations proceed

Drab November a day lost in thought

A fight in a dark alley
and an accordionist from Ukraine
who plays the toccata and fugue

A hundred years pass since the first
war's conclusion
We await the second

Night and fireworks
and refugees landing on a stony beach
and Aphrodite who triumphantly

calmly strides the waves of a sea
dark as wine

And shopping malls where
contented humanity moves
both left and right

And we still don't know why Ovid was exiled
from Rome and why Rome
forgot everything
and why we forgot
everything

Name Day

Once, when I was still a student, I gave my mother
a book about Brueghel (the father) for her name day
and after a week I took it back, claiming I would
need it for my "work" (she laughed at me).

These days though modernity invades
even cemeteries—not far from her grave
they've placed a candlemat, that's right, a candlemat,
a metal post, a machine dispensing candles,
you just toss two or three obols in the slot.

The name day for *Ludwika* came again, I went to that city,
not a city now but a tropical forest of memories
and my childhood spoke to me, every street
spoke, sang, maybe even shouted, yes,
shouted, talking about what had been and what
no longer was, and also about those I used to know.

I wasn't sure how to pray for the dead
in such tumult, in the shriek of recollection.
I placed a pot of small chrysanthemums on the gravestone
and understood only going home
that this had been a prayer, this momentary hesitation.

Then I also realized I hadn't brought a pen
or pencil, I couldn't write down

what had happened, luckily I was saved
by the gas station cashier, she made me
a present of a used gold ballpoint pen
and an unused sheet of A4 paper.

I quickly started scribbling and while I scrawled
clumsy sentences my friends appeared out of nowhere,
Charlie Williams and also Tomaž Šalamun—
I thought Tomaž would particularly like
the idea of the ballpoint at the gas station.

I truthfully explained: "but that's how it was, really,"
and I heard an answer: "really,
what does it mean really?" (they spoke together,
laughing, although I know their *aesthetics*
had radically differed in the past).

And nothing had changed, nothing had changed;
it was already dark when I got back to Kraków,
the last days of August, but still quite warm,
summer remembered its youth, even the night
was warm and elastic, nothing had changed,
armies of stalactites slowly grew in caves
and satellites stammered surveilling the earth,
and nothing had changed, nothing.

Errata from Many Years Past

for Julian Kornhauser

I happened upon the errata
to a volume from many years past:

"Line 15 on pg. 13 should read:
Not trumpeter at trumpeter no trumpet oh black mother
The printer sincerely apologizes to the readers for this error"

Alas it's too late
to change a thing
The trumpeter turned up but was misplaced again
We can't find the trumpet
The printer offers no apologies
The printer is no more
Mama has died
There aren't many readers either

And we're not at all sure how to live
so as not to require errata
We don't know if such a life is possible
and if errata can really be free of errors